Grace and Vince

by David Nguyen
illustrated by Jennifer Emery

Core Decodable 64

Bothell, WA • Chicago, IL • Columbus, OH • New York, NY

MHEonline.com

Copyright © 2015 McGraw-Hill Education

All rights reserved. No part of this publication may be reproduced or distributed in any form or by any means, or stored in a database or retrieval system, without the prior written consent of McGraw-Hill Education, including, but not limited to, network storage or transmission, or broadcast for distance learning.

Send all inquiries to:
McGraw-Hill Education
8787 Orion Place
Columbus, OH 43240

ISBN: 978-0-02-145104-3
MHID: 0-02-145104-4

Printed in the United States of America.

2 3 4 5 6 7 8 9 DOC 20 19 18 17 16 15

Grace shopped at Civic Center Mall. Her cell rang. Vince called.

"Do you have a pencil?" Vince asked.
Grace smiled. "I do."

"Can you make a shopping list?
Ice, rice, spice?" asked Vince.

"And citrus drinks and cider?" Vince added.
"Can you get them all?"

"I can't," Grace grinned.

"You do not have cash?" asked Vince.

Grace's pencil fell.
"I do not have the hands!"